PRAISE FOR *OTHER SIDE OF BROKEN*

The poems in *Other Side of Broken* by Kimberly Casey are gritty, boldly honest, and deeply personal, while also possessing a universal resonance and profound insight into the human condition. Casey recognizes and skillfully uses the cycles of daily routines as the scaffolding upon which hangs the grand drama of life. The poetic images cycle through this book in the same way, revealing the nonlinear nature of breaking, being broken, and the journey to the other side.

—Jerri Hardesty, CEO and Publishing Editor at New Dawn Unlimited, Inc.

It is the poet's job to translate the human condition on the page, and Kimberly Casey exemplifies that. In her second collection, *Other Side of Broken*, Casey explores the ways in which we build, break, and rebuild in the face of love, loss, and self-discovery. What does it mean to mother without children? How can a broken relationship teach us to heal? How can the beautiful, blooming routine of nature give us steady ground to keep on living? These poems remind us that tenderness is required for our hearts, our bodies, our relationships, but also our memories. Casey's emotionally stirring and achingly real poems give us a blueprint for starting again, and to see our wounds as evidence of a life fully lived.

—Ashley M. Jones, Alabama Poet Laureate Emerita

In *Other Side of Broken*, Kimberly Casey fearlessly and tenderly probes the wreckage of relationships—and lives—shattered by addiction, and a body wracked with chronic pain and illness. And yet, turning to nature and the animal world for solace, she continues "digging for the bone of joy." Casey's grief-wrought poems brought me to my knees again and again—but they also left me with "the taste of hallelujah on my tongue."

—Therese Gleason, author of *Hemicrania*

OTHER SIDE OF BROKEN

Kimberly Casey

Riot in Your Throat
publishing fierce, feminist poetry

Casey, Kimberly
1st edition.
ISBN: 979-8-9947052-0-9

Cover Art: Steph Flier
Cover Design: Kirsten Birst
Book Design: Shanna Compton
Author Photo: Mike Matthews

Riot in Your Throat
Arlington, VA
www.riotinyourthroat.com

CONTENTS

BROOD

"Poetry, like water, seeks its own level."
—Marvin Bell

We use a water level to set posts for the deck in February.
The yellow box squealed when the water perfectly balanced,
an obnoxious reminder. The deck frame now soaks, abandoned
in the May showers. Inside, a new water heater,
new mini split, schematics for a new septic system. Sometimes
need gets in the way of want.   Mother's Day weekend
I child's pose in the yard, a backstretch turned prayer.
Brood XIII cicadas sing shrill psalms. A cry for life.
On the news,   another picture of a pile of children's
bodies among the rubble. I touch my hand to my abdomen
shifting scales under my skin. I blame a bank account,
a body, a history of addiction and mental illness.
But still my womb seeks its own level.   I mother
my dogs. My community. My climbing team. I mother
the version of my younger self who still takes control
of the puppet strings of anger from time to time.
Cicadas have so much to say for such a short life,
and I too, sometimes scream my way through days
others could call beautiful.   Call level.
My eyes turn red with the newness of sight.
I too, am shedding a second skin, an armor of my own design.

A FEARED LANGUAGE

The doctor calls me stable.
Maybe able to bring one weary
animal warmth yet still I shed
everything out. A birth
here would be deemed miracle.
Barren is a feared language
perhaps too antiquated for my age.
Call me barn instead, all open doors
unable to keep anything in,
covered in red and dying straw.

THE DOG SPEAKS

Other times / I am left with the taste of hallelujah on my tongue / Nails trimmed to the quick / I am digging for the bone of joy / buried deep in the red clay / fervently working the earth / Forgive me all this mud / forgive the way I swallow / each breath like a last meal / I am working to avoid the relentless shatter of myself / again / to become light as a feather / and soft as a feather / and never ever bored or stiff or slant / Pavlov's bell tricks me into hunger / but also / tricks me into hope / Mind all this drool / I am praying again / Everything smells like heaven / can't you taste it?

DANDELION

In conversation with "Acorns" by Phillis Levin

It is the season
of sowing and
my yard is full
of only
clover and dandelion.

Before it blooms
to a seed head
bracing
against wind,

the bright breath
of a child

eager to
scatter snow
across the spring lawn,

it begins as a mirror
to the sun—
yellow florets stretch
to reflect light
until nightfall.

What resilience
to avoid every passing breeze
until it's ready

to gently let
its future children fly
into the world

with such confidence
they will continue
to thrive,

once a crystal globe
now without snow

the stem let go

newborn seeds searching to root
but it is what her body knew to do.

O tell me how to live with a body
that can't let go of its seeds

dying
to leave a legacy behind.

HER FIRST DEPLOYMENT

In conversation with "Hope and Love" by Jane Hirschfield

All winter long my father prayed for my mother.
I do not know what drives a man back to church
after three decades, do not know if the customs,
the ash fingertips on the forehead, create comfort
for him, for how he missed her touch—

or the clean house, the full fridge.
As the frogs sing under the stars, I know
god can be the biggest wound we carry.
He folds one fist into the mitt of his palm,
a worn cloth polishing a stone smooth.

LANDSCAPE

The young conifers' ego exceeds its age,
sapling limbs spilling upwards into sky.
I sit on the forest floor, stare up at needles
as they float across wisps of cirrus clouds
with each breeze exhaling from the west.
Broke from travel, I still bought
a new turquoise necklace and matching ring
from Sadie Green's Curiosity Shoppe
to wear to my aunt's funeral. Now, I fumble
fingers along their silver wire framework.
Protection and healing are what the woman
behind the counter spoke of. I told her
my aunt always brought me here on my birthday
to shop for something extravagant. What possesses me
to press the bruise of the past? I do not want
to exacerbate the pain of grief. Perhaps it is a fear
of forgetting, or of being forgotten.
Trees' root systems connect under the earth
creating a chain of communication to send
distress signals about drought and disease
and to share nutrients to those in need.
The sapling is in the shade, but is receiving
strength from its elders, from the soft moss
and mushrooms. I hear my mother start
the new tractor to dig her pond deeper,
hoping to hit a natural well and make
an oasis where my brother and I
once built teepees of branches and bedsheets,
where we later buried stolen sticky bottles
of Mike's Hard and Twisted Teas.

The engine echoes off the granite slab
at my back, dances at the gaping maw
of the cave to my left. I leave
the ring among the moss, another totem
for all the ages I've ever been,
new roots twisting in with old growth.

DAWN

I still wash the dishes by hand
despite the new house's new appliances,
dishwasher included. We used to ask my father

why he didn't upgrade our childhood home:
We made two perfectly good dishwashers right here!
he'd bellow and gesture at my brother and me.
We'd shake our heads and return to the sink.

Now I keep the tradition alive. The clean
while you cook mentality my mother handed down
sometimes gets lost on difficult days,

but even when dishes pile high I prefer to be reminded
of what my hands can accomplish:
take a dirty thing and make it clean again,

the scum at the bottom of a pint glass,
the ceramic bowl with chili stains,
the bent ice cream spoon, all scrubbed.

Send soap bubbles into the air, touch
a cluster to the top of my dog's nose.
The pile disappearing, the grime gone,

memories popping like soap bubbles
breaking open.

OIL SPILL

When the power went out
father stepped from the shower
with soap in his eyes, tripped,
and hit a fist through the door.
Pulling his hand back clean,
he kicked the base of the door
for good measure, a second wound
opening beneath his foot.

Putting away groceries,
after dropping one egg
accidentally, he began
plucking out each orb
and throwing it at the tile
until the carton was empty
and the floor was littered
with shattered shells.

Changing the oil
a bolt dropped into the pan
his hand whipped to catch it
but knocked the pan instead,
oil spilling over the edge
running down the driveway.

I was a child
eager to learn,
to spackle and sand
to make something
broken look new,

to sweep and mop
the smallest fractures,
to be ready to catch
the darkening drip
before it spilled
staining everything.

LEASH TRAINING

Tough instruction spit through gritted teeth. A dare to tug away again.
A quick thumping against the walls of my throat, cannon
sounding the alarm of an inherited violence.

I never saw myself as a mother. Posed as a midwife for a friend,
sliced through her tough placenta with a serrated blade,
tossed it into the blender to make her a smoothie.

The dog yanks the leash again as another car passes,
nearly launching us both into traffic. A neighbor stares
as I sit on the sidewalk, my right hand loosening its grip
on the collar, tears on my cheeks as I relax the sharpened strike
of my left. I hold his wide face in my palm. I try not to yell.
I just love you too much to lose you, I say and kiss the top of his muzzle.
What more do I have to do to prove it?

CIRCUITOUS

My grandparents had nine children,
twenty-one grandchildren.
My grandmother had arms like freight trains—
carried all of us passengers,
but I was the only one my grandfather held.
9 pounds 8 ounces of playdoh,
he wasn't worried about hurting me.

Age five, moving to the country all I wanted
was to play around the construction site
to prove to my older brother I could do
everything just the same as him.
We would play in the cement foundation
down the bare board stairs to catch
daddy long legs and let them crawl up our arms—
he thought I would get scared, but I never let him see.
Then we would pull off their legs one by one.

Age ten, I considered myself a handy woman.
I thought knew my way around tools
and I wanted fix what had been broken.
I learned to plaster holes in the walls,
measure mesh screen from knuckle to knuckle
remembered always to sand down smooth
clear coat of paint on top.
There were things I knew I could fix.

Age fifteen and there he was—
red hair, red cheeks, red nose,
bottle of booze in a slush puppy cup,

sightseeing a town we thought we knew
but then the red left his face.
I knew they were not just freckles on the
insides of his marionette elbows.
He became the first of many lost boys.
There are things I learned I could not fix.

A week before my eighteenth birthday
I crumpled a fence with my mother's car,
drunk and reaching for my cell phone,
stunned by the force of the airbag and
unable to recognize this moment's truth
as a passive attempt to end it.

Age twenty-eight, I was learning to believe
not all loves leave in a casket.
The southern sun lassoed me
tight around the ring finger
during a lunar eclipse in the Smokies
and for a brief time I was able to imagine
I deserved some soft forever.

Then it was autumn again. Thirty.
My love and I filled drink dispensers
with water and sweet tea
as we filled our home with friends and family
to watch us wed in the backyard
under the mulberry tree.

How could I know grandfather would
pass in three days, weighing less than his age?
That within the same time, my husband

would have his first beer
in over a decade, calling it a toast
to a very special occasion?

How could I guess three years from now
I will be watching my aunts and uncles
crowd around the kitchen table
to share stories about Chicopee High
and summer camp.

I will be divorced
for longer than I had the ring.
He will be one month sober.
We will both be trying
to walk in two directions.

Under the mulberry tree,
our friend kept the ceremony short and sweet,
not enough time for too many tears.
My heels sank into the soft earth below.
Blue jays chirp, pulling the last of the berries
from the branches overhead,
filling themselves for the winter to come.

THE WAY WE WEATHER

When it rains, the dog claws the bathroom tile
searching for a more significant shelter.

We call to him, spin a record.
Dylan drowns out the thunder.

The dog sniffs the grout regardless,
whimpering,

drool hanging from fleshy, downturned jowls,
teeth chattering.

We read about thunder shirts, wrap him
in that old sweater, an ace bandage,

anything to make him feel held. But his chest
still shivers with each exhale.

We cannot fix his fear. Memory
pulped through the sieve of time

still carries its history
deep within our tissue, our muscles.

We gather in the small bathroom together,
place his soft bed in the center of the floor.

He paws for an hour and we sit with him,
watching bits of fabric pull apart.

As he settles in, he stops shaking, and the bellowing thunder disappears, turning into his soft snoring.

DROUGHT

The hill soft slopes then drops off steep
spotted with stones sticking out of the soil
to use as a staircase to the secret swimming hole.
Sneakers skid and scuff the rocks but never stumble.
The trail is littered with leaves, fallen not for the season
but for the lack of rain, burnt love notes curled up
and forgotten in the firepit. The slip and crunch
underfoot briefly distract from his broad back,
a crisp white shirt I've stared at for an hour as he leads,
unaware if anyone has fallen behind. The pool reflects less
sky now that the water is broken by more boulders,
black surfaced and cratered like coral. He is perched
on a stone in the center of the water, staring
into the forest. I timidly take off my shirt and shorts,
tugging at the edges of the brittle elastic of my bathing suit
and examine my own signs of drought—
the trail of black hair down the center of my stomach,
blistered toes and overgrown nails, split ends,
the swell of my abdomen, hormones holding water
weight pooling in my center. I press on my belly,
imagining a waterbed shifting and sloshing
under intertwined bodies eager to expose
every inch of themselves. But the bloat stays
anchored to my uterus speckled with cysts
and scar tissue. I enter the water alone
and the pressure on my spine lifts. The ripples
travel towards his gaze, wake him from his trance.
I wonder where he goes. When he looks at me
my body is gone beneath the water,
submerged up to my chin, so he can no longer see

the sick parts of me. The sun pulls a cloud
to cover itself. I stare back at my shirt
balled up at the shore. He smiles and splashes
droplets dark and shimmering. The cloud
sighs and plays along, releasing light rain
that rustles the tops of the trees, trickles down,
disappearing beneath a blanket of moss.

CITRUS

His fingertips smell like citrus.
The hollow bowl of skin,
set on the countertop, the scent
diffusing into the kitchen.

I sweep these remains into the trash.
I used to eat half a grapefruit every morning
next to avocado toast topped with a fried egg
after a bitter cup of black coffee.

On our honeymoon in Kauai,
we toured the botanical gardens
and our guide explained the origins
of the orange fruits found around us.

The pomelo is the base citrus
for most others. It is a nonhybrid,
resilient. We joked about growing
a tree in our backyard at home.

Orange bottles had been growing
in the cabinets for the last few months.
Wedding planning, a degree, a new job
heightened my heart rate, kept me from sleep.

May cause drowsiness, dizziness,
changes in the rhythm of the heart.
May increase the effects of the medication.
These effects may last up to 3 days.

It stands to reason the increase
could help—can I feel sad when I'm asleep?
Maybe he wants me to taste this fruit,
tempt my heart into changing its beat.

He cracks his first beer in 12 years
on an island we know we'll never visit again.
We clink the necks together. I still believe
people can change.

I have a panic attack
that jolts me from dreaming.
The sun has barely risen, just enough
to offer the sky a small orange rind.

HOW TO SURVIVE THE RELAPSE

Leave fresh water on the nightstand.
Remind yourself it's not
as bad this time, without
remembering last time.

Make manageable rules—
don't bring beer home,
no drinks after your shift,
keep a clean house.

Start drinking coffee again.
Hold the warm cup close to your cheek.
Watch every sunrise
from the east corner of the sunroom.
Try to stay grateful.

Tell your mother.
No matter how much your voice shakes
she'll still speak soft on the end of the line,
reminding you what a home should feel like.

Believe there is a way to find balance.
Buy running shoes, encourage
daily hikes with the dogs,
home cook meals every night.

Feign surprise when it doesn't work.
He has already let this long-lost love
slip up his spine into his brain stem.
You will never be as good as drunk feels.

Leave the way you forgive yourself—
slowly first, then all at once.
Gather your things as you gather yourself,
the way the pond in your new backyard
becomes more sure of itself
after each storm.

PARTICULATES

A germ suspended itself in the air between us
giving off the glow of leaving before either

knew we needed an exit.
The fever engulfing us grew,

but not in that once newlywed-heat way
all sweat and gasp and blush, no,

now our marriage has bubbled to blister.
What does a love language mean

when we have already stopped speaking?
Does our zodiac sign tell us

how to apologize, how to dismantle
the bricks we've built up between our bodies?

The rain is getting inside again.
We cover everything in plastic:

the furniture, my books, his guitar,
but we forget to shelter ourselves.

I wish I knew how to be his
umbrella, his coat,

a thick cowl scarf around his neck
to trap enough warmth to survive winter.

DECAF

The coffee he left on the bedside table
is cold by the time I get to it. The fan breeze

taking the heat from the cup, from my bones,
steam rises and is ushered away

as autumn leaves brown,
gathering forgotten on the back porch steps.

It's been days since I could stand
for long enough to sweep without

needing more pain pills to keep me upright.
He leaves me notes stuck to the fridge,

next to the medicine cabinet, on the chest of drawers.
I imagine his fingers sweeping over the paper,

thumbing the edges of the post it notes,
tucking his tongue between his teeth while he writes.

I've forgotten the feel of his fingers.
When I smell ink, I think of him.

OVERGROWN PATIO

Springtime weather shakes lose
the forgotten potted porch plants' leaves.
We never bring them in on time.

Drinking turned drowning,
what was once rooted now rots
with the relentless winter rain.

He says he wants to stop,
doesn't want to force
another funeral on me.

Cold cut stems and browned leaves
turned inward against
each other's decay—

we'll be better next year.
There's always next year.

DISAPPEAR SLOWLY

The pug's tiny teeth grate against the aged antler
shaving away invisible flecks, cleaning up with her tongue.
This is how it is to disappear slowly,

little by little, never enough for anyone to notice.
My aunt says *you look so healthy now*
as I flatten the mashed potato piles on my plate.

Grandmother used to fill the dining room with food
and we'd fix plates in our own time, sit where we found a chair,
take as many deviled eggs as we wanted, eat dessert first.

She disappeared quickly, loudly,
with a cough that shook the house as it tore tar from her lungs,
a glass of wine vibrating next to the recliner.

Once, I blew through my sneakers on a run.
I swore they were fine the day before, then
my toes were touching cold concrete.

The free cases from the brewery used to stack high
next to the spare mini fridge in the garage.
These days I cannot keep it a quarter full.

Time resizes my memories. Wasn't I just sitting
on my grandmother's lap, playing Scrabble and sipping chocolate milk?
My plate is empty. I am asking for seconds.

WHEN YOU SLEEP WITH SOMEONE ELSE

it's not because you don't love your husband
but because you love him so much you can't keep
letting the lack of sex stop you from sleeping
curled in close to him anymore. You're afraid
he's stopped wanting to touch you since the surgery
to take the cysts away from ovaries,
the scar tissue from tilted uterus. He's afraid
to hurt you again, so he kisses your forehead,
turns away, turns on talk radio and disappears
into dreams. He snores within minutes.

You tiptoe downstairs to the kitchen
sift through the fresh blueberries, tossing
the burst and bruised ones, mixing the rest
with flour, sugar, and eggs to make muffins
for the morning when you will finally be in bed.
You lick the spoon, snack on a cookie
made the night before, eye the orange
pill bottles on top of the fridge that stay
mostly full now. Scroll through
your phone looking at pictures of your nieces
until the oven beeps.

The decision to have an open relationship
is one you and your husband talk through
for months. You are still best friends,
still in love, still want to spend nights
falling asleep with his fingers in your hair,
waking up to kiss as he sets a cup of coffee
on your bedside table. You still go on dinner dates,

try, but he slips inside and softens
so you roll over with your legs around him
kiss his eyelids, run your thumb along his jaw.

He presses his hand into the small of your back,
tilting his head to kiss your collar bone, and tells you
he'd be okay with it. Maybe it would take the pressure
off him so he could just enjoy the moments
wrapped around each other like this.

When you gently ask if the alcohol is a factor,
he blushes crimson, mumbles about the last time,
the last woman who tried to love him into sobriety
and brushes you off, tucks the sheets around himself
unconsciously, a second nature separation.

The first time you open the door
to an unfamiliar mouth, you won't love him any less.
You won't love yourself any less.
You'll dig out the expensive lingerie
crumpled in the back corner of the top drawer
put it on and eye yourself carefully in the mirror.
A person you used to know will stare back
sultry and fearless. You'll take off the lingerie again,
dress comfortably, drive to meet with a man
you can trust with your timid trying,
drink one extra beer so your cheeks stay blushed
unable to show your embarrassed nerves
as you unwind your wrap dress to reveal
cotton panties and a mismatched bra.

This new man will ask about the scar later,
after you've stitched yourself into his skin
with your tongue tip, after he's parted your legs
and lifted you onto a table, hard and shameless.
You tell him a clipped lie about appendicitis
as you reach for your clothes. He stops you
and kisses this closed threshold to the broken parts of you.
He can tell you're lying, but he doesn't pry,
so you turn towards him,
open yourself up again.

INVASIVE

I am picking at the weeds again.
Winter may be unwinding from my ribs,
but the corners are crowded with clover
and poison ivy. Why is it so hard to grow
hearty tomatoes, strong stalks of beans
but the burweed spreads to spike our heels
each spring? Why is it so hard to keep
running, climbing, training and eating clean,
but the bottles still fit snug in my grip?
I am trying to keep the right things alive
and remove the rest without ruining
the whole plot of land. Some things linger
in the soil, no matter how much the rain
washes away. I keep adding compost.
Build a new trellis. Feed the plants nitrogen.
But I can't keep my eyes off the fence line
for fear of what could be growing underneath.

FOUR POST

Nighttime knocks at my bedpost
doesn't care how tired I am
wants me to get up
kick off the night
a sweet tooth craving
typewriters fingers along
his gently expanding sternum.

Don't you want to unwrap and unravel tonight?
I ask myself in the bathroom mirror
already knowing his answer
in my saltwater stomach
gnarled hips split with the agony
remembering bottle rockets.

I don't know exactly when I stopped
belonging to this body
but now I want to sever myself from it
in search of sleep.

I used to late night stumble
through the door to kiss
sweet sweat from skin
unflinching, unfeeling
wanting and taking.

Now his body lies
turned and tucked away
too tired from the trying and the failing,
like softness is some marital sin
no matter how much you brush it off.

Now my body is a shook highway overpass
quaking and breaking, freezing and thawing,
and who could love an overpass?
Who could love something so run over?
So tread marked?

EQUINOX

The 22nd of September is a magnet—blood and iron, pulling and pulsing.
There was no church, no bells, but there remains resonance in certain sounds:
Leonard Cohen, blue jays in the mulberry tree, sweet tea pouring into paper cups,
dozens of sparklers sizzling at once lighting the path home,
the drag of dress shoes along the grain of unfinished, historic hardwood halls.

Never one for vanity, adorned only with clip in extensions and mascara,
a $100 dress, thrifted heels with backup Chuck Taylors at the ready—
perhaps an omen I was always bluffing, playing a character.

Six years ago we celebrated with all our friends in our forever home.
He was sober, smiling, I couldn't have imagined the precipice approaching.
A new anniversary this year. The one of him finally trying to dry out a second time.
Phone calls to urgent care and scouring over affordable online programs,
lining up friends and neighbors to check on him while I was out of town.

Topaz in its natural element is clear, but it is colored by its impurities
to make it more appealing to the eye. It is a symbol of love and affection,
the stone that celebrates a 4th wedding anniversary. What colored our marriage
still lingers. I keep answering the phone long after signing the papers
because each ring is a talisman, a reminder we will always be intertwined.

SIGNING THE PAPERS

Spouse 1 Last Name Prior to First Marriage

I have always been my mother's daughter,
despite the distance, she calls
to tell me about the new hiking trails
she has carved from the earth,
ready for my running shoes.

Number of This Marriage

If you kiss a falling tree
alone in the woods
and no one hears you whisper
I love you,
does it really make a sound?

Number of Children in This Household

Over 1,500 species have been recorded
to eat their young, on occasion.
Does that first bite
feel like a cyst rupturing?
My teeth are sharp
but my womb is hollow.

Date of Separation. Date of Final Decree

I can remember calling Maya
while driving into work
crying because the last thread severed.

Now we are wearing masks.
Thanksgiving is coming.
I am not good at admitting
failure.

Legal Grounds for Decree

I cannot tell you who you are,
but I know where you've been.
You're standing in a mirror.
You're both here, and back there.
Cheers to the cycle,
turned upside down and back
around again. Do your hands
miss my body? Or do the cans
keep them company?

Decree Awarded To

The hot cup of coffee
held cradled between both hands
on the timid, screened-in porch.
The steam rising up
to meet a vast new sunrise.

ON WATCHING *JOKER* WHILE FLYING TO A FUNERAL

Painting tongue with white makeup, the Joker welcomes those who wronged him into his home. I watch from this stiff blue seat, stealing moments to look out the window at the wing. My backpack sits under the seat in front, full of plastic pill bottles, shaking along with the vibrations of the plane. Joker writes "the worst thing about having a mental illness is people expect you to behave as if you don't." I try to act normal, though the six-foot suit next to me keeps watching me scratch my forearms. I take Ativan and drink a Bloody Mary, staring at my cell phone. My anger exists under my skin—I keep trying to claw it out. My jaw clenches. I said I would try to sleep on the flight, but I have not slept in weeks. I keep dreaming of the boys I have laid with lain into coffins. It is becoming more fact than nightmare. I think Joker paints his tongue because he knows the thing he is trying to cover lives within. My therapist says I deserve to be vulnerable, but I just keep swallowing paint, hoping to coat the inside of me. My ex-husband says he doesn't want to be another funeral for me to attend. His words slur. Trust becomes a traitor. I love the broken bits of people and I want to honor each edge, but I can only slice the side of my fingers so many times. I tattoo memorials onto my body and understand I will never know their pain. I run every day. I lift weights. I drink too much. I try to put myself into places of pain I can understand. Joker dances down the stairs as he starts killing the things that hurt him. I want to keep these things that hurt me alive, even if they hurt me again and again and again. Because they'd still be alive. Even in all their ugliness. Even with needles and nicotine gnawing at their nails. Even with their blemished and bruised skin. Even with their faces falling deeper into their skulls, smiles made of scars.

WHAT WORDS ARE LEFT TO USE?

In conversation with "What It Looks Like to Us and the Words We Use" by Ada Limón

I show her photos
from the solo trip.
Pronounced cabins
along the lake
soft pine logs
old enough to prove
they can
withstand decay,
a waterfall
of stairs
to the shoreline,
brawny
yet diminutive
against the cliff.

Mom says
They look
like splinters
waiting for a sole,
or a palm to run
down the length
of the warped rail.

I say
I'd hate to live
there in winter
and I think of breaking
a shovel through ice
in the driveway
when my mother asks

Do you really believe
you'll be
happier alone?

And I say *No.*

I believe I can be
grounded, stable
steps against
the avalanche.

And she says
You are
your mother's
daughter.

And we stand
motionless
on her back deck
among the falling
fattening flakes,
the swaying pine,
the circling dogs,
a Northern Hawk Owl
my father
named DeMinimis,
asking *Who?*
and I refuse
to name
any blame.

So instead,
we look
into each other,
ask how,
her crow's feet
working their way
into my own
forced smirk,
tear ducts
heavy though
we know neither
would release—

tears unspoken,
inherited,
ours.

SMALL JOYS IN THE MIDST OF DIVORCE

1. All the art is exactly where you want it to be.

2. The new rental house, settling with small snaps and pops in the middle of the night, eventually becomes less scary.

3. One month in—you've already cried in every room of the house. Sometimes it has been for a joyful reason. Sometimes can be enough to make all the other times worth it.

4. Now you can jump start a car and change the battery all on your own. With a slight assist from Google.

5. You live close enough to work to coast with the gas light on till the next paycheck comes.

6. Have the beer. Brew the tea. Read the book. Watch Netflix. Shut off your phone. All without permission.

7. You didn't get electrocuted changing the light fixture.

8. You declared victory over cockroaches in the great battle of the apple bag.

9. Your parents' RV just barely fits under the low-slung powerlines in your driveway, but they can pull in close enough to plug in and recharge.

10. This bed, built with your own hands: sturdy, comfortable, covered in your favorite pillows. Even when you can't sleep you still feel rested.

11. You can split the neighborhood—walk the dog on the side of a sunrise sky, run two miles on the side of sunset.

12. The phone rings less, but the people who stay love you fiercely—bring you lunches and play board games, and do puzzles, and only talk about it when you want to talk about it.

13. You feel stronger push-mowing the yard, looking back at all the places you've been, seeing the rows for growth ahead.

NEW AGE ARCHAEOLOGY

The boat-tailed grackle crackles a caw across the shimmering silver pond.
I clear my throat on the deck, the first noise made aloud this afternoon,
calling back to the birds across the wind. Today, I existed in the digital
only, keyboard clacking and emails whooshed off to clients and coworkers,
bouncing between accounts and reports and spreadsheets and analytics.
Now there is no screen. I take my fingers and massage my temples,
remind myself I am more than a box, a name in the bottom right corner.
I pace the new grass in the backyard and unearth charms with my toes
left behind from past residents: bottle caps, six shells, two tent stakes.
The summer heat has baked the red clay bone dry, the dirt hollowed.
Four pennies, twelve pull tabs, bent and rusted nails of various sizes.
I want to leave less behind, build a legacy out of absence instead of excess,
but I cog my way through most days, clock in and cash out. The birds watch
as I bend down to dig up a chipped aqua tile to add to my pile. I say names
out loud, warm up my voice, remind myself of what else has been lost
to the dirt. Crumpled candy wrapper, toy police car, spent bullet.

FISHING OR FALLING IN LOVE

The line has to be tough enough to handle the weight / but thin enough to not be noticed by the fish / The knot needs to be precise / tough without tails to tangle / Try out different lures / brighter when the water is clear / deep greens and blues when the storms have kicked up the dirt / Cast toward the edge of the shadow / Fish worth catching dance along the edge of light and dark / Count to 20 / let the lure sink to just before the bottom / Reel slow / but flick your wrist quick / Pull back at the bite to set the hook / and reel hard / Let it come to the boat / tired and giving up the fight / When you grab its lip / pull it into the boat / he is smiling at the size of the fish / or the way you proudly pull out the hook / hitching your voice up an octave / tell the fish thank you / gently dipping it through the surface / watching it disappear back between the swirling seaweed below

SUBTEXT

Over burritos and Jarritos with my ex-husband
we talk about his trip to the folk art museum in Georgia
avoiding the drunk Instagram story
posted with his new girlfriend.

He excuses himself to the bathroom
and when he returns down the steps
he doesn't appear to have noticed
the second toothbrush by the sink.

We are moving through something
we swore would always haunt us.
We are putting our toes in the ocean
on the other side of broken.

STILLNESS IN SEPTEMBER

Every plant is still damp from last night's rain
but even at just past sunrise the humidity is pulling, pulling.
A hornet teeters on the edge of the glass in the sill
regrowing green onions, sips deeply.
The neighbor's rooster crows with delight over a new day
before the heat stifles him into silence.
The dog naps on the upended chair cushion
running in her sleep, leaving small smudges
from paws covered in red clay. If you are to love me,

know this: I often need an early, slow morning.
Decaf and a notebook, no sounds, just the sunrise,
phones still inside on the charger. My feet will get muddy
drenched in dew. Sometimes I brave the back deck
in only my underwear and an oversized tee because who cares
what the neighbors think. Sometimes, here, I will cry
over the aging dog, or the sounds of the cicadas, or
the relationship ended a decade ago, or last night's movie
about a shell with infinite wisdom, or how beautifully you sleep
because all these things grow vines within me
that are shimmering all at once and I honor them
when they decide to twine the valves of my heart.

I reckon with not having children but I try to mother every moment,
capture it like a poem and show it in a mirror, remind myself
it is beautiful in every simple way. If you are to love me,
know this, I will second guess myself often
because I am always trying to pass a test of my own making.
You'll gently remind me to relax.
I have a hard time sleeping, but I love to try.

I keep water on the nightstand, but I barely touch it.
Sometimes, I howl at the moons in your eyes.
I flinch, even when you don't expect me to,

but you won't always see it. I'll remember
all the things I've said to you and all the things
you've done to me and I'll battle with building resentment.
If you are to love me, know this. I need to feel the breeze
of the ocean once a year or I'll get cranky and age too quickly.
Sometimes I'll want to party with you till 2AM
and sit on the stoop under the stars
but mostly that sounds exhausting. Mostly I am just waiting
for you to hold me. The grass grows. The morning commuters
crank their engines. The dew is drying out.
Nothing stays still for too long.

THE ESCAPE

Twilight. A timid new love. We're driving again. I can feel the grain of your words on my skin, the rasp of your voice scratching the dusk. We will never be smooth. You are a rough almond, popped into my wanting mouth. My tongue is salty. An agate wrapped in silver swings from the rearview mirror of the Ford Escape, above the car radio, sweating static into the humid night air swirling between the open windows, down I-65 east, aiming for a new home.

I must remember to call my mother and thank her. I never do that enough. Her forgiveness melts the phone line, sage honey in my ear, down my cheek, a tear. I miss living close enough to hug her, but I keep her wisdom like a stone worked smooth with the worry of my thumb.

I shift my weight, adjust my spine to lean in closer, not with a defensive bend, instead leading with a heart unfurling, open to the wind. I want to press my lips to the dashboard. I want to pray to the smell of gasoline.

Carry me away. I promise I won't try to take all this darkness with me this time. I promise it can just be us trying to be better than before. I am hopeful, but I am a woman of my time. Let's keep our word. Let's shake out our secrets, a blanket full of sand after this beach day of dumb luck. Let's send out the line, let's see what we can catch. Let's drive even further into the night, into a new Atlantic sunrise.

GRIEF IN A NEW ROOM

You are sleeping on the wrong side of the stairwell
grieving an ex from a decade ago you thought you healed from.
This isn't the room where you used to paint the walls
and now your dreams are upside down and backward
and he is still alive and just down the street and
you're going to go visit him at his dad's after the holiday.
Go back to sleep in this room. Keep him alive
in your nighttime mind. Let him linger there
among the Christmas movies and jingles,
simmering in the brain stew with you
in an old house with a new room
where you've never kissed him before,
but also, where you've never had to lose him.
Wake up. Don't correct your subconscious.
Call his dad. Tell him how much you miss them.
At least that hasn't changed.

HOW TO GET BACK UP

Learn to tie new knots / the kind that hold fast / the kind that slip / Pull weeds in the garden with your bare hands / Keep them busy / Check the seedlings every day / Water them / then water yourself / Run / On days you feel like you can't / do it anyway / but let yourself complain the whole time / Stop at Sonic on the way home for a large Reese's Blast / call it balance / Call your brother / your best friend a few states away / start doing crossword puzzles / Write a poem a day for a month / share them / especially when the poems are bad / Remember / vulnerability is most powerful when shared / Dive into your work / close the computer no later than 4 PM / Walk the dogs every day / especially when it's raining / You were made for all kinds of weather / Keep opening the windows / Keep opening the doors / Keep opening

HYDROPLANE

I think we moved too quickly.
The storm was still circling overhead.
The paperwork was just finalized at the courthouse
and I truly tried to embrace my eager freedom
but he was already there, fishing pole in hand
ready to ignite a new adventure.
We propelled toward each other too fast
and so, we lost contact with the pavement
and spun out of control. Of course
it couldn't last. The tread on my trust
was worn too thin by the last road I wandered
and he still carried fuel in lines from last summer.
The rain has ended and the puddles have
nearly dried. I'll drive slower next time.

HELD

When I invite you into my bed,
it's more than what you may think.
Sure, it can become its own open plain,
but everywhere there are expanses
waiting for the reaping. Here,
I am welcoming you into a holy space.
The prop for elbows eager with prayer.
The nest for a bloated body, twisted
around a hot water bottle and a snoring pup.
Where I call my mother on weekends,
talk about the ill aunt and the lost uncle.
The first place I greet each day,
a slow morning with a cooling cup of coffee
under a warm blanket. Let me lie here a bit longer
before I remember how to be unkind to my body,
before the office or the bills or the phone calls or the news.
Here is where we connect. I kiss the tip of your nose
and tell you the ways the day scared me, and you remind me
of my muscles, rubbing them with lotion and lavender.
Yes, sometimes I pull the computer on my lap
to continue the workday, but you remind me to close it,
bring us ice cream, put on a scary movie.
I read, and you watch videos on your phone
and interrupt only when something is really really funny.
We add more blankets just to toss them to the floor,
honoring our bodies' ever-changing needs.
Cradle my throat with your palm.
Let my hair drape over your shoulder
as I kiss the crook of your neck.

Yes, here we can explore, ignite, yearn and please,
but we can also unravel, drift off to sleep
knowing we are held.

WILDERNESS INSTINCT

Palms stained purple, sticky blackberries and summer sweat.
Dirt shelters under his fingernails. I want to take my teeth to them,
mine for minerals. My hair is splayed out over the backpack,
a sham on a makeshift pillow. The limestone huecos, millions of years old,
were formed from expanding magma seeping into stone, cooling,
crumbing away, now a home to an orb weaver and her tidy dinner.
We don't dare disturb her. Followed the blue blazes on the oak trees
a few miles to get here and we don't want to make any trouble.
We know we're visitors, playing house in something else's home,
making jungle gym out of their front yard. I am building the blocks
in my brain on how to trust him again. Letting him spot me
on a highball boulder, ready to catch me if I slip. Allowing him
to belay me in the gym on the 5.12 I've been projecting on top rope.
This new love has never dropped me but has abandoned me once before.
He says he wants to try again. I reckon with forgiveness.
With reopening doors. And I can picture it.
Chirping good morning over protein pancakes
and homemade chai lattes. Kissing him every time he leaves
for work, every time he returns home, a breath exhaled.
I feel the beg of my body around his lean arms,
the rugged rubble of his abdomen. The magma within me
has had time to cool but there are hollow huecos left behind.
I have found stasis in the simplicity of solitude.
He brings a complicated chaos. A hunter with the foil of a doe.
A blackberry-stained second first kiss.
The orb spider slowly weaves another round.

CIRCUITOUS

The wraparound deck secured tightly to the exterior of the roundhouse dome
the skylight with its spokes of oak and glass pane pie slices
the swirling whirlpool tub under the center
for a view of overhanging boughs and stars—
I am seeing so many circles on this trip to the Smokies.
The spiraling ramp around the observatory tower to Clingmans Dome
the severe switchbacks rounding the mountain peaks
the straw swirling the ice around inside my melting cold brew.
I used to love seeing these circles,
marked the moon phases forever on my skin
as an ode to the cyclical nature of things
how what once felt good can come back around to greet you,
if you just keep pushing onward. But sometimes
it starts to feel like you're just wearing a rut into the earth beneath you.
The last time I was here, six years ago,
I accepted a simple circle, a ring offered honest and timid
and try as I might, despite the resizing and recalibrating
it fell off for good. I have now been longer without that ring
than with it. I wear another round rut into the earth. Since,
I've only let the round sound of love leave my lips to one, but eventually,
they left too. Another round worn into the earth.
Another friend dies an avoidable death. My dog limps with age. I take calls
from friends who can't put bottles down. Another circle. Another cycle.
In all this looping lately I've spent too much time looking down at my feet.
Sitting on the porch swing with a notebook, I push myself into the noticing.
Yes, the old choruses repeat. Life and death, love and loss,
abundance and lack. Circuits we continue to complete again and again,
though the currents of our lives continue onward to new connections,
new elevations, new surroundings.
Some cycles are inevitable but what becomes new is how we approach them.

The rain this week has made the creeks current into a crescendo
weaving itself around rocks to wear them smooth. Later
the sun will crest and pull that water back to the sky,
each droplet dancing upward. I can't imagine them
rolling over with groans of *Here we go again.*
Instead, they approach the clouds like a lost lover
arms open, ready for the best part of their favorite film.
Looking back along my own winding rut
I can see the life it has weaved through,
mountains and valleys, some cautious treads, some worn deep
like a path around a playground slide,
climbing up eager just to experience the fall again.
Yes, I remember now, can you hear that,
the sound of a love calling you back to bed,
or the sound of a parent saying they're proud,
or the song you only sing when you're alone and you feel like dancing,
or friends wishing you a happy birthday,
celebrating another rotation around the sun.
That sound. Your favorite part. It's getting louder.
It'll be here soon. Be ready. Try like you never failed.
Remember everything.

MOONFLOWER

Take off your heavy coat. Dress yourself in bits of lace.
Ignore the clock, the beeping of the trash truck in the street,
the scratch of the squirrel dining on acorns in the ceiling.
Focus on your breath, the way you release
the weight of each day from your heavy breast
with each exhale. When you imagine who you are,
who you are becoming, I hope you paint yourself true,
tender, lonesome, vibrant, a container
of blood and milk and sweat swirling in sinew
hardening into enchanted minerals. Spill yourself
onto the bedspread, a canvas, an O'Keeffe creation,
a gentle body blooming, a moonflower most alive at night.
Forgive yourself for not sleeping. Be still,
honor the space you inhabit, the imprint you leave,
the heat that lingers after you ease yourself into a new day.
Your bamboo robe with loose threads
slouches down your shoulders as you watch the sunrise
while drinking a cup of coffee on the front stoop,
a cigarette in your hand.
A moonflower wilting is still beautiful.

RUNNING THROUGH CEMETERIES

There is a moment when you are running
when you are only moving for the sake of moving
where your lungs feel close to collapse and one more mile
is a plant wilting in the palms of your hands
but you remember being told to run tall
to drive roots into the ground with each touch of sole to earth
and somehow, you keep going,
round the next bend to see something beautiful.
Or terrifying. Or bland or unique or small or selfish or extravagant.
But the point is you get to see something new,
something yet unnamed. Even here on hallowed ground
where the ghosts of a dozen dead friends
and the rivers of dozens more washed-out relationships
create a cold current in the air around you,
the sun peaks a hazy ember, the frost falls from the flower petals.

REASONS TO BE GRATEFUL FOR FAILING

To fall asleep nested between two snoring dogs.
To wake before the sun and allow my body
to move and feel strong. To sleep in and steep
hot chai tea and almond milk. To cry in the movie theater
because an ending was so beautiful. To learn to catch fish
only to throw them back. To grow my own food
and can it for the winter. To tear my knees and hands
on limestone and granite for the sake of reaching new heights.
To exercise muscles I once didn't know
the names of. To build a family only to watch it
break, to feel that loving again would be impossible
and then doing the impossible anyway. To feel
my new lover reach for me in the morning and squeeze,
sniffing my hair. To experience loss and be able to grieve
instead of being the cause of grief. To see the scars
fade, the knives dull, the bottle of pills expire.
To get a text that he is three weeks sober.
To plan a wraparound deck to sit on in the summer.
To camp in the woods without any distractions.
To have a rest day and feel like I'm worthy of it.
To know you. To write this. To bloom.

ACKNOWLEDGMENTS

Gratitude and appreciation to the following journals in which these poems first appeared:

COMP Journal: "Signing the Papers," "Particulates," and "Her First Deployment

Hare's Paw Lit: "Citrus"

Out Loud HSV: A Year in Review 2022: "Disappear Slowly" and "Grief in a New Room"

Out Loud HSV: A Year in Review 2023: "Running Through Cemeteries"

Out Loud HSV: A Year in Review 2024: "Brood"

Southern Women's Review: "A Feared Language"

THANKS

It is such an honor and a privilege to work with Riot in Your Throat again, and I am endlessly grateful to Courtney LeBlanc for her support and encouragement. Courtney is a gem in the literary world and it means so much to be part of the incredible cohort she is growing through this press.

To my Pacific MFA writing community—thank you for all the inspiration. To Sarah Elkins and Therese Gleason Carr for the writing prompts that lead to these poems. To Melissa McKinstry for helping me find the throughline and nurture this manuscript from a haphazard pile of poems into a meaningful retelling. To Zach Furlough for reading through this manuscript, telling me it was ready, and that the only edit was to kick it off with Marvin—you were right. I know you'll love to see that in print. Thank you for believing in me before I was ready to believe in me.

I am forever indebted to my past instructors at the Pacific MFA program for teaching me so much about balancing writing and life. Thank you to Kwame Dawes, Dorianne Laux, Joseph Millar, Marvin Bell, Ellen Bass, and Mahtem Shiferraw. My time learning from these greats is something I will cherish for my whole life.

To the Out Loud Huntsville community, I am grateful you continue to allow me to grow with you and learn from you. This community is everything to me. Thank you for showing up for each other month after month, being brave and vulnerable and honest.

To my best friend Borka, thank you for letting me talk nonstop about the content of these poems on our runs every single week.

To Steph Flier—you're a creative genius and your artwork being on the cover of my book is one of the greatest gifts I have ever received. Thank you for collaborating, for sharing your vision, for being so endlessly inspiring. I know reading this will make you uncomfortable—deal with it.

To my parents, who drove across the country in an RV in the middle of a global pandemic to help me move into a new apartment and make sure I was okay—I am so lucky to have you both. I know what real love is because I know you two. Thank you for your care, support, and encouragement.

To those people who helped inspire these poems, you know who you are, and you know I love you always. Thank you for the millions of beautiful moments, even the ones that hurt. I am who I am because of you.

ABOUT THE AUTHOR

Kimberly Casey is a poet and community organizer located in Huntsville, AL. She is the Founder and President of Out Loud Huntsville, a nonprofit organization dedicated to inspiring community outreach and activism through written and spoken word. She received her MFA from Pacific University in 2021, and published her first full length collection, *Where the Water Begins*, in 2021 with Riot in Your Throat. She is the Editor for the *Out Loud HSV: A Year in Review* anthology, and she serves on the board of the Alabama Writers Forum. She loves rock climbing, running, and spending time in nature with her two pups. Learn more at kimberlycpoetry.com

ABOUT THE PRESS

Riot in Your Throat is an independent press that publishes fierce, feminist poetry.

Support independent authors, artists, and presses.

Visit us online:
www.riotinyourthroat.com

RIOT IN YOUR THROAT BOOKS

Sarah Beddow *Dispatches from Frontier Schools*
Kathryn Bratt-Pfotenhauer *Bad Animal*
Kimberly Casey *The Other Side of Broken*
Kimberly Casey *Where the Water Begins*
Sonia Greenfield *All Possible Histories*
Elizabeth Hazen *The Sky Will Hold*
Brett Elizabeth Jenkins *Brilliant Little Body*
Melissa Fite Johnson *Green*
Melissa Fite Johnson *Midlife Abecedarian*
Hadley Jones *Devout*
Hilary King *Stitched on Me*
Frances Klein *Another Life*
Courtney LeBlanc *Exquisite Bloody, Beating Heart*
Courtney LeBlanc *Her Dark Everything*
Jill Michelle *Underwater*
Shilo Niziolek *Little Deaths*
Laura Passin *Borrowing Your Body*
Laura Passin *We the Destroyers*
Sara Quinn Rivara *Little Beast*
Laurie Rachkus Uttich *Somewhere, a Woman Lowers the Hem of Her Skirt*
Karen J. Weyant *Avoiding the Rapture*

www.ingramcontent.com/pod-product-compliance
Lightning Source LLC
LaVergne TN
LVHW041233150826
845673LV00008B/2375

9798994705209